The Hard Questions

Also by Susan Piver

The Wisdom of a Broken Heart

*Start Here Now: An Open-Hearted Guide to the
Path and Practice of Meditation*

*The Four Noble Truths of Love: Buddhist Wisdom for
Modern Relationships*

The Hard Questions

100 ESSENTIAL QUESTIONS
TO ASK BEFORE YOU SAY
"I DO"

Susan Piver

A TarcherPerigee Book

tarcherperigee

an imprint of Penguin Random House LLC
penguinrandomhouse.com

Originally published in paperback in 2000 by Tarcher Books
Revised and updated in 2021

TarcherPerigee with tp colophon is a registered trademark of
Penguin Random House LLC

Most TarcherPerigee books are available at special quantity
discounts for bulk purchase for sales promotions, premiums,
fund-raising, and educational needs. Special books or book
excerpts also can be created to fit specific needs. For details,
write SpecialMarkets@penguinrandomhouse.com.

Library of Congress Cataloging-in-Publication Data
Names: Piver, Susan.
Title: The hard questions: 100 essential questions to ask
before you say "I do" / Susan Piver.
Description: [Revised and updated edition] | New York:
TarcherPerigee, an imprint of Penguin Random House LLC, [2021]
Identifiers: LCCN 2020055730 (print) | LCCN 2020055731 (ebook) |
ISBN 9780593418871 (paperback) |
ISBN 9780593420676 (ebook)
Subjects: LCSH: Marriage. | Communication in marriage.
Classification: LCC HQ734 .P72 2021 (print) |
LCC HQ734 (ebook) | DDC 306.81—dc23
LC record available at https://lccn.loc.gov/2020055730
LC ebook record available at https://lccn.loc.gov/2020055731

Sonnet XII from *Full Woman, Fleshly Apple, Hot Moon: Selected Poems
of Pablo Neruda*, translation © 1997 by Stephen Mitchell

Designed by Patrice Sheridan

Printed in the United States of America
ScoutAutomatedPrintCode

For Duncan.
You're the one.
_____

CONTENTS

Foreword

—

ix

INTRODUCTION

–

1

CHAPTER ONE

Home

—

45

CHAPTER TWO

Money

—

56

CHAPTER THREE

Work

—

64

CHAPTER FOUR

Health and Food

—

68

Contents

CHAPTER FIVE

Family

—

74

CHAPTER SIX

Children

—

79

CHAPTER SEVEN

Community and Friends

—

88

CHAPTER EIGHT

Society

—

91

CHAPTER NINE

Spirituality

—

95

Afterword

—

99

Acknowledgments

—

103

About the Author

—

105

FOREWORD

Loving is a journey with water and with stars,
With smothered air and abrupt storms of flour.
Loving is a clash of lightning-bolts,
And two bodies defeated by a single drop
  of honey.

—Pablo Neruda, from Sonnet XII

I chose to open this book with these beautiful lines from Pablo Neruda nearly twenty years ago, when the manuscript for the first edition was taking shape. At the time, I was just about to get married. I thought I knew what they meant—something about growing closer and then more distant, giving and withholding, loving and estrangement, and that enigmatic "single drop of honey," the unbidden moment when everything simply melts and a new layer of love is revealed.

Whatever I thought these words meant then, they mean even more now. After experiencing so many ups and downs, mysterious bursts of new love and equally mysterious disappearances, the passing of loved ones, and the blessings and difficulties of aging, all with the same partner, I'm grateful to have the opportunity to revise this work in light of that greater (and still-evolving) understanding. I hope this new edition of *The Hard Questions* will invite an even deeper conversation between two people considering a most potent commitment.

Some parts of this revised work remain the same: questions according to certain categories in our lives (home, work, children, and so on), the spirit of the suggested dialogue, and the intention to use these questions to lead to a commitment one might actually be able to honor. There are differences, too: added questions about the place of technology in our lives, new questions that reflect changes in how we live (or don't live) physically together with partners, and cultural shifts in the way we think about finances, nutrition, and spirituality. I removed the chapter with questions about sex because answering questions about sex places the conversation in a purely conceptual context. Conversations about intimacy may be quite valuable, but the intimacy itself is a better guide for a couple than any questions I could put forth. I added a whole new chapter called "Society" to cover increasingly fraught political and environmental issues and also to take into account issues of inclusivity and cultural biases. These questions aren't meant to put my political beliefs forward, but to elicit conversation about your own.

At this writing, asking the Hard Questions has inspired (and probably mystified) hundreds of thousands of couples. The ideas behind this book—that loving someone and loving your life together don't always seamlessly connect; that feelings, desire, and personality change—have apparently resonated with many people. They, like my partner and I, were looking for a practical, accessible tool to create intimacy beyond romance. It is my profound hope that this book has helped them in some small way to create their own version of love.

Since *The Hard Questions* was first published, I've received countless emails from couples who have used this book for that purpose. Most began the conversation because one partner thought it would be a good idea and the other partner readily/eventually agreed. Others received it from a friend or parent. They looked at this small, innocuous volume and began blithely answering questions. And, exactly as happened with Duncan and me, at some point or another one or more of the questions turned into a marathon conversation, complete with yelling, tears, stunned silence, and, almost always, reconciliation. This is so great. Not to say that I hope to provoke disagreement, but the idea of couples taking a chance on exploring hopes and fears together makes me happy. I know that doing so creates the basis for ongoing intimacy.

In the more than twenty years since we've been married, I've only grown to appreciate the process of inquiry into self and other more. The questions themselves are what provide the value, not necessarily the answers. To truly inquire of your beloved's state of mind and heart requires that you offer them a large degree of space—room to be themselves, speak the truth, take a chance. Too, incredible closeness is required: endless attention to the details of each other's mood, what kind of day they had, the dream they dreamed last night. Noticing your partner at this level, keeping your inner and outer eyes trained on them without blinking, enables you to see the world from their point of view. You get so close that you can see the world from inside their mind—and therefore know exactly what questions to ask, and when. Keeping distance *and* shadowing their every step—this is the dance of marriage.

♡ **When we first** answered the questions, during the glorious (and crazed) time of planning our wedding, like others, we agreed, disagreed, and drew a blank on an equal number of questions. During the ensuing years, many of our answers changed, even if only for a few hours, days, or weeks. There were times when I felt certain that our love was dead. There were times when I was equally certain that Duncan had been my soul mate for all my previous lifetimes and would be for all the future ones. Some nights I would get in bed after he was asleep and put my hand on his chest to feel the rise and fall of his breath and the beating heart underneath. I would cry at the preciousness and impermanence of those sensations, and my own heart would expand and expand with equal parts love for this cherished being and pain at the anticipation of our inevitable, though hopefully distant, parting. Other nights, after arguing about something big (where to live) or, more likely, small (the importance of using an electric toothbrush), I would get in bed and turn my back on the unknowable oaf who dared call himself my husband—what a jerk. Over and over, we've experienced phase after phase of distance followed by closeness followed by distance, etc. We've been consumed by love, anger, boredom, and all manner of passion for each other, positive and negative. Throughout all these phases of emotion, attraction, friendship, and estrangement, one thing has remained constant: our willingness to inquire into the truth of the other's heart. As we've been able to ride the waves of feeling, no matter how pleasurable or painful, we've remained companions and partners. The moment we took our eyes off the reality of our shifting hopes and fears to gaze instead at the way we *wished* reality looked, we found ourselves estranged from each other. Over and over, we've learned the lesson of staying awake to each other's shifting energies through the simple process of asking questions—and being willing to listen wholeheartedly to the answers.

Throughout, I have seen again and again a single truth that makes the Hard Questions worth exploring: *They are going to come up anyway.* It is better to answer them consciously, lovingly, honestly, and during a peaceful time rather than to have an argument about them later. If you agree on the answers to certain questions, celebrate. If you disagree, celebrate! You will have learned important things about each other before they have a chance to become points of contention.

I wish you all the strength and softness you need to answer the Hard Questions genuinely and honestly. Here's to love and its endlessly surprising power to heal, embolden, and expand the heart's capacity beyond what I could ever have imagined.

The Hard Questions

INTRODUCTION

—♡—

When my husband, Duncan, asked me to marry him, I immediately tried to break up with him. We had been together five years, through his divorce, my move to another city, career upheavals, and trying to make things okay for his hurt, loving young son. I loved this man. I loved our relationship. But I couldn't imagine promising to love him—or anyone—for the rest of my life. How could such a thing be possible? Every relationship I had ever had up to this point, romantic or otherwise, showed me that *feelings change*. If I stood in front of the world and promised to love him, I would start our partnership with a lie.

With great trepidation, I suggested a month of separation to think things over. I wanted to reflect seriously. I mean, wasn't I meant to be an adventuress, a seeker of truth, a lover of beings, a captain of industry, all in this lifetime? My orientation in life had always been toward experiences, accomplishments, and growth. How could these things mesh with being a wife? How could I follow my heart and soul and still guarantee a commitment to this one single, solitary person, with all his uniquely glorious, utterly divine, lovable ways *and* his confounding, awful, frustrating qualities? It seemed so . . . domestic.

Upon further reflection, I realized I was holding some fairly dark assumptions about commitment. Somehow, I believed that once married, I would simply cease living on a certain level. While till now I had been free to roam the earth as my home, marriage would be like confining myself to one room. No! Never! Not ever! This compromise I would not make, not for love or money or threats of a lonely old age.

After our month apart, after these thoughts and realizations, Duncan and I got together for the weekend. We were both quite nervous. Our lives were about to go in this direction or that. I was ready to lay it all out, without expectation of any particular outcome. As I recall, I made some speech about how he could never expect me to be a traditional wife, about my independent and nonconforming nature. He listened quite openly and then, in response, gave me a little box shaped like a heart. Inside it were a rock and a feather. Duncan told me, "The rock is me. You are the feather. Fly. Let me be constant and steady. We can hold it all in one heart."

All my words were gone. I felt how much I loved him, saw how well he knew me, and, shock of shocks, that he was willing to be in a relationship with me, as I am.

As had happened before in this intense relationship, just when I thought we were about to hit a wall, my love for Duncan expanded to yet another level I could not have imagined. For the first time in my life, it dawned on me that perhaps it was possible to marry, and that marriage would enhance my life rather than constrain it. I realized that the fear I had been holding, the fear of not being accepted for who I am, was immense, old, deeply embedded. Duncan didn't help me get over it, but our relationship allowed me to see it. This—seeing yourself and your beloved more deeply—is at the heart of intimacy.

We spent the rest of the weekend in a loving cocoon. When we parted, I knew I couldn't let this relationship go, that I loved Duncan with all my heart. But still I couldn't reconcile with the marriage vow of constancy. And then I came to a simple realization that enabled me to say yes to him. I realized that, no matter how much I might love him in any given moment, I couldn't commit to loving him like this for my whole life, or to sustaining any single emotion of any kind toward anyone for the rest of my life. I would be doing him a disservice by suggesting that I could.

But what I could commit to, what I longed to commit to, what I believed I was capable of was to *act lovingly* toward him for the rest of my life.

To act lovingly is a complex and mysterious thing. It is not a matter of being nice. It begins with the ability (and willingness) to be honest, with ourselves, with each other, with life, from moment to moment, and dealing together with the emotions that may arise—be they love, hate, boredom, jealousy, ecstasy, apathy, or any combination thereof. In this way, moments of intimacy accrue. I can tell you now, looking back over our life together, these are the moments that actually create the fabric of our relationship. The truth is, romance always ends. This is not to say that it becomes impossible—certainly there are romantic moments and experiences—but romance ceases to be the context that defines the relationship.

Love Affairs and Relationships
Are Different

When it comes to commitment, what begins as a love affair must somehow find its way to become a relationship. Love affairs and relationships are not the same thing. (For some reason, no one tells us this.) We expect our love affairs to easily morph into relationships and our relationships to somehow remain love affairs. The truth is, this is rare. The trouble begins when we try to force a love affair, something amorous, passionate, and dreamy, into a relationship, something that centers on everyday life. Love affairs take us out of the ordinary. Relationships are crafted by the ordinary. Weirdly, our cultural depictions of love seem limited to the love affair variety. But the love that can arise within a relationship, over time, with care, breath by breath, kiss by kiss, is just as powerful. You can flash-fry a meal or cook it low and slow and in either case end up with something delicious—but the love that is built over time is not glamorized. It should be. No love affair will support you through the death of a parent or as you age, share your joy in the new flower that finally blossomed in the garden, appreciate what you endured to get a college degree, or hold you night after night in bed. Love affairs are fueled by surprise. Relationships, by knowing. Emotions and passion keep a love affair alive. Pushing past your limits in love are what perpetuate a relationship.

The Four Qualities
That Support Relationships

What makes a relationship different from a love affair and what can keep it alive? I've discovered that four qualities are needed.

<u>1.</u>   **Honesty.** This may go without saying, but poof, I said it anyway. Honesty is not about blurting your thoughts the moment they enter your mind. That's silly. Honesty begins with knowing the truth yourself, or with realizing that you simply don't know what is true at the moment and more time is needed. If I ask how you feel about me, your answer could be *I love you*, *I don't know*, or *I'm torn—just not*

sure. Whatever answer is accurate is the right one to give, but if you are not sure because you are trapped in what you "should" feel or afraid to admit something to yourself, you may give a very convincing answer, but it will be misleading.

To know yourself well enough to be honest requires a commitment to moment-to-moment self-knowledge as the circumstances of your life shift and change. This capacity is good for you, certainly, but it is also great for your partner. The truth is, what scares us most about others is not their irritating (or worse) habits—it is to sense a lack of awareness on their part. Unconsciousness in another is what actually frightens us. When I am hurt by my husband, there may have been an inciting incident, but when I feel he is not seeing me or is unwilling to listen to me—or listens but does not understand—then I become afraid in some primal way. The commitment to self-knowledge that gives rise to honesty is one of the two foundational qualities that make a relationship work. You can have a fabulous love affair with someone who doesn't know how to be honest about their inner life, don't get me wrong. But if you think you will be able to have a relationship, that's another story.

2. Good manners. I realize that may sound prosaic, but the other foundational quality without which a strong relationship is simply not possible is good manners. I'm not talking about knowing which fork to use, I'm talking about the kind of good manners that result from thoughtfulness. If you have a guest, for example, you think about what they might want when they arrive and try to have it for them. You consider the sleeping arrangements and try to make them comfortable. If your guest goes out to visit a sick relative, you think about how they might feel upon returning and are ready with a kind ear or a cup of coffee. This is what I mean by good manners. If you are with someone who won't actually *think* about you, again, you could have a fabulous love affair, but the chances of a good relationship are pretty close to zip.

3. Compassion. Compassion is often misidentified. We think it means being nice. Compassion and being nice are not the same! Somehow, we've gotten the idea that to be compassionate, we have to basically babysit everyone. True compassion is far more intelligent than that. Sure, sometimes it means being sweet and offering a hug, but other times it means saying nothing, and still other times it may mean getting really angry. We don't know what the most compassionate thing to do is unless we are paying attention to what is actually happening (rather than to our own ideas about what is or should be happening). To pay attention in this way to our partner, we need to assign a certain status to them. That status? *The person you are in a relationship with has equal importance to yourself.* When I first realized that, I will confess, I was shocked. What?! I thought this relationship was about me and "getting my needs met." Okay, sure. But it did not end there, much to my surprise. There was another human being right next to me who had his own feelings and needs. Each time I prioritized myself, I lost sight of him. When I prioritized him over myself, I felt lost. At some point, I realized that no matter how divergent our opinions or feelings might be, each one's was as important as the other's. Without thinking of each other this way, you may not be in a relationship but some kind of transactional agreement where I win this one and you win that one. Of course, this can only mean one thing: everyone loses. I'm not saying compromise is not important; it is, vitally so. But if our relationship becomes a scorecard due to lack of willingness to give equal weight to the other's concerns, well, something important is missing.

4. **Courage.** Many people who say they want love don't mean that exactly. We are actually looking for safety, shelter, a respite from life's difficulties.

I hope my relationship will be just that and I hope yours will be, too. However, it is not likely to be so all the time. When relationship problems arise, it is totally normal to feel threatened by them . . . *maybe we won't be able to work it out.* In reaction, you might try to argue the problem away, double down on your efforts to be non-threatening, or, if all else fails, just ignore it. (That latter is my personal favorite.) It is just too scary to look closely at certain issues. Understood! However, courage is required if you want the relationship to continue to deepen. Weirdly, relationships never stand still. Whether a little or a lot, they seem to always be growing closer or more distant. Stasis is rare. Love can't be locked down, and if all you want to experience with your partner is love, I'm afraid you're in bad shape. But fear not! There is something even better than love. All you need to discover it is . . . courage.

The truth is, love will come and go. It begins and ends, begins and ends. However, there is one quality that seems to have no end, none whatsoever. You can never run out of it or come to the end of the road. It is called intimacy.

Rather than looking at everything that happens between you and your loved one as a chance to give or get more love, you could look at it as a chance to become more intimate. How much more can you reveal of yourself? Invite from your beloved? How deeply can you know and be known? This is a journey without end, a commitment you can make truthfully. All it takes is courage.

♡ **After my crisis** of faith in love, marriage, and self, and after contemplating the nature of commitment itself and then deciding to marry, all sorts of demonic thoughts began to plague me: What if Duncan wants to live somewhere I hate? What if I wish we had ten times more money than he wishes for? Is he really okay with spending lots of time with my family, or was he just saying so? In another fit of insecurity and doubt, I wrote down these questions. The list grew. As I wrote, I realized that there was a third presence in our relationship, that it wasn't just he and I, and that this entity was the thing that could cause our marriage to fail—not any lack of love, passion, or agreement about what the marriage commitment should be.

This entity? Our life together. The thing that we would create to house our love. As I pondered this, as I remembered past relationships, I had a realization. I mean, I had been in love before, but now those relationships were over. Why? What would make this one any different? Then it struck me like a lightning bolt. *Just because you love someone*, a voice inside my head said, *does not mean you will love your life together.* Wait. What? No one ever told me this before. I suppose I just assumed that loving someone automatically meant you'd love your life together. That's how it always looked in the movies. Then I realized that what caused my past relationships to fail was never lack of love—I still love them all, truth be told—but some sticking point about creating a shared life. I knew Duncan and I loved each other, but how much did I really know about how he envisioned our life together? How much had I shared with him? When you're dating, you don't exactly talk about how much money you have, which holidays are important to you, or what your kid should call me. But these are the things we tend to argue about, not love.

What were Duncan's feelings about home life? My relationship to his son? His relationship to my parents? Our bank accounts? I had to admit, I had only assumptions and hints.

The questions continued to come. I wrote them down. And one by one, Duncan and I answered them, together. Some questions took days to answer. Some took a moment. Others had no answer, and that in itself was informative. In every case, we learned something about our relationship and each other. We were delighted, appalled, infuriated, and/or mystified by each other's answers. It was an extraordinarily fruitful and bonding experience, one that had nothing to do with whether we agreed, disagreed, or were stumped and everything to do with knowing each other better. The questions took us everywhere, from the cold, gray heart of disagreement and misunderstanding to the sweet, warm belly of loving intimacy—all of which was great preparation for marriage itself. When we stood up together in our marriage ceremony, we knew, as much as we were able, what we were saying and whom we were saying it to. When I looked into Duncan's eyes and said I would be his partner, I felt it was the most honest promise I had ever made, one offered from the very center of my heart, directly into his.

How Answering the Hard Questions Can Help You Make a Powerful Commitment

In this book, you'll find many of the questions Duncan and I answered, plus more, gathered from friends, strangers, relatives, and, in this version, from people now in their twenties and thirties who are considering what commitment means to them. There are differences I could not have predicted when this book was first published: the prevalence of social media and its role in the way we connect with others, the vast political divide that could now spell "deal breaker" (whereas before it may simply have meant heated discussions around the dinner table), shifts in the meaning of spirituality and religion, changing values around home and possessions, the rise of gig culture and remote work, the need to confront racism and cultural biases, and environmental concerns that have grown sharper and more pressing. This revised edition has questions that seek to take all of this into account. Too, the openness to post-traditional couples has blossomed. Though many questions are no different for the LGBTQIA community, additional questions are needed and I have done my best to add what may be useful—and to remove the tyranny of gendered pronouns without adding wordy weight. If you don't see your preferred pronouns represented as often as you like, I ask your forgiveness. I also tried to rephrase questions to remove cultural biases I had been unaware of (and am still learning about).

If you desire a committed relationship, passionate yet also down-to-earth, this process of asking questions can help you achieve it. If you are looking for ways to honor the commitment of life partnership with someone you love, without giving up who you are and what you dream, this book is for you. And, if you feel, as many do, that *I don't want to get divorced and I want to be as clear as possible about what I am saying "yes" to*, answer the Hard Questions.

We enter marriage offering the best of who we are: our deepest feelings, our best intentions, our greatest hopes, full of generosity and affection for our partners. But we fall in love and decide to live the rest of our lives together without realizing that loving each other and loving our life together *are different*. This book is about envisioning your life together with love, care, and mindfulness. It is about skillfully balancing the crazy wisdom of love with the grounded practicality of making a life together. It is about the middle road, the constant, meaningful interplay between these two poles, loving a person and loving the life you create together. Strong marriages exist here, between the fire of intimacy and the ground of pragmatism.

How to Answer the Hard Questions

An important note right up front: I'm a white cisgender woman. I carry certain cultural biases. Since this book was first written, there is increased awareness about recognizing and repairing the imbalances created by these biases. I've done my best to make the questions more open and less biased, but I know there will be moments where I have failed. If you would be kind enough to point out these failures to me, I would be grateful. You can reach me via my website, openheartproject.com.

In the past, there was little need to create a shared

vision of married life. Tradition may have ruled the day; you married someone from your town who shared your religious upbringing, and gender roles were less fluid. For those contemplating marriage now, a conscious effort is needed to create a shared vision. Anything is possible. Nothing can be taken for granted. There are almost no cultural models for us to look to. Often, traditional religious values no longer support our relationship. For many of us, our divorced parents can't offer a model to emulate. How, then, to create a mature view of relationships that is also unique to each couple?

There is no technique, no gimmick, no class, no easy answer. The only way that I have ever found is to know and reveal yourself to your partner— relentlessly, and with great discernment.

The Hard Questions helps create a shared view of life and a deeper knowledge of yourself and your beloved. It can be used throughout the life of a relationship; answering these questions ten years into it is as valuable as answering them ten months into it. The questions can be used by binary, non-binary, or non-gendered individuals and are not predicated on any particular faith or religious belief. You can believe whatever you like and still answer the Hard Questions. Whether used as an ongoing tool or as the basis of a single conversation, within the context of a committed relationship or as a tool for self-knowledge, the Hard Questions can help lead to a deeper level of intimacy.

It is important to recognize that each of your answers contains important information about who you are, what you believe, how you were raised, and what you value. No matter how simple the answer may appear on the surface, once you scratch the surface, you will find a reservoir of powerful emotions and deeply held beliefs. You may or may not be conscious of just how deep it goes. When your partner gives an answer that sparks anger or fear in you, it is important to put those emotional responses on hold, even if just for a moment. It can be hard to do this, I know. But if you can redirect your attention away from your reflexive response (well-founded though it may be) and toward your partner's internal logic, you will both benefit tremendously. No matter how odd or inappropriate or silly you find your partner's response, I guarantee that, to them, there is a powerful, important set of reasons for it, reasons that *matter*.* The work is to understand your partner's internal logic.

This is not a simple undertaking. To talk about life views with a partner can raise all sorts of fears. It is a very vulnerable thing to do, and when we feel vulnerable, we are less tolerant of each other. Here are a few simple suggestions for having an important conversation when the outcome really,

---

*This suggestion does not include answers that may indicate problems of abuse or addiction. These are different categories, and the suggestion to understand first and react emotionally second does not stand. These factors change the context for a conversation like this. I don't want anyone to think, *Some author lady told me I should not have strong emotional reactions* when abuse or addiction are present. Again, those are different situations. Please consult experts, friends, or family about how to proceed.

really matters without falling into a rabbit hole of fear that prevents you from speaking clearly and listening well.

First, and most important, is to understand what is meant by "to listen." Trust me, if you can get good at this, you can pretty much be good at relationships, period. I learned this definition of listening from a friend, fellow writer, and underground genius named Catherine MacCoun. She said, "Listening is when you stop thinking your thoughts and start thinking mine." Whoa, Catherine. That is brilliant—and not at all what I had been doing when I thought I was listening. Rather than listening *to* the other person, I was listening *for* something: I was picking through their words for things that might give me hope or cause me to fear. On one hand, that is a sensible thing to do. Words are important. On the other, when your ear is attuned to what the words being spoken might mean to you instead of what they mean to the one who is speaking, the one you are speaking to is yourself. I'm not sure what that is called, but I'm pretty sure it's not called "listening." When we sift first and attempt to understand second, the meaning gets lost.

It's great to experiment with this capacity, beginning with nonthreatening conversations. Can you let go of your thoughts about what is being said and instead simply hear what is being said? If you can get even 10 percent better at this, you will discover that it is a profound superpower, one with the capacity to generate connection, deepen understanding, and resolve conflict. DON'T TAKE MY WORD FOR THIS. (Or anything, really.) Try it yourself and see.

When it is your turn to speak, I offer you four mini-questions to ask yourself before you open your pie-hole. This may sound complex: four things?! But, for real, after a time, you will see that you can consider all four points in a few moments.

1. Is it kind? This is a loaded question because we somehow think "kind" and "nice" are the same

thing. *They are not*. What is kind is what will deepen the connection between you and another person and create more love. Sometimes that involves sweetness and light, but sometimes it means keeping your mouth shut or even getting angry (if, for example, you see your beloved about to engage in self-destructive behavior and need to break through their confusion). I want to be sure you hear this suggestion not as an invitation to be a sap but to be real. That is ultimately the most kind thing you can do.

2. Is it necessary? Meaning, is it on point? Rather than throwing all the words you have at a certain topic, can you pare them down to the words that actually matter, that address the issue at hand?

3. Is it timely? You may know what you want to say and have a perfectly prepared statement in answer to a particular question, but is this the right time to offer it? Is my partner actually listening to me or are they still wrapped up in their most recent thoughts—or their own hopes and fears? Did they just come home from an exhausting day at work? Are you about to go to sleep and you know they love (or hate) before-bed conversation? That kind of thing.

4. Is this the right place? Your words may be kind, necessary, and timely—but if you are having a discussion on the sofa versus in a car versus at a sporting event, the conversation will go a particular way. I'm not saying one environment is better than another, just that environment matters.

♡ **No matter when,** how, or where you answer the Hard Questions, this process is powerful. It will blow away half-thoughts and fantasies. It will uncover your hiding places. It asks that you accept it all, that you open to truly knowing your beloved. It asks you to show yourself, allow yourself to be known. This is not for the faint of heart, but neither is marriage.

Don't try to answer all the questions in one sitting. It may take days, weeks, or even months to fully answer them. Each time you are ready to discuss some of the Hard Questions, choose a place that feels right to you both. Some couples like to discuss questions over dinner. Some like to do so on a walk or on the weekends. Duncan and I first began discussing them on long car rides. The important thing is to minimize distractions.

If it is useful, you can set a time limit on the discussion, such as, "Let's devote thirty minutes [or one hour, or two days] to focusing on these questions and no more." It can be very helpful for some, especially introverts, to have parameters for such conversations.

First, spend some time contemplating your own answers to the questions under discussion. Do your best to become clear about what your real feelings are. You may be certain of the answer or you may not be sure—either way is fine; what is important is to know what is true now.

Each question is meant to be answered by both

of you, one at a time. Allow each person to answer fully, without interruption. You can sit close together, holding hands; apart across a table; or use the phone—whatever enables you to focus and concentrate is what you should do.

Try to listen completely, with as little judgment as possible. Instead, allow yourself to become curious. Curiosity is actually a form of fearlessness, when you think about it. It takes courage to let go of your hopes and fears in order to truly take in the other person. Open up more and more space in your own mind and heart for your partner's answers. Your own judgments and responses, while vitally important, are not the point right now. Trust, really trust, that they will still be there when you need them. (They will.)

If there is agreement between your response and that of your partner, you could write out the shared answer in a notebook or shared word doc. This is not about memorializing your answers in a contractual form. Rather, it is a way to create a snapshot in time of who you each are right now, what you long for, worry about, intend, and are unsure of.

When you have finished answering the Hard Questions, you will have important answers about making your life together happy at this moment in time. Whether you have agreed, disagreed, or drawn a blank, you will have learned a lot about each other. Feel free to revisit the answers or change them together anytime. Life changes and so will the answers to the Hard Questions.

It is wonderful when you and your partner agree on the answer to one of the Hard Questions. But one thing our culture doesn't teach us is that it can be equally wonderful when you and your partner disagree. We tend to fear disagreement; our minds come up with so many stories about what disagreement means. *We're not right for each other*, we think. *My life will be made miserable by this person. Or I will have to become someone I'm not in order to make this work.*

But if we work with our minds, we can arrive at

a place where disagreement means none of these things (barring deal-breaker questions; see page 36). We are accustomed to believing that discomfort is bad, should be banished and eradicated by whatever means available. It's true that discomfort is . . . uncomfortable . . . but if we can find a way, within ourselves and together, to hold off, even for just a moment, from running from discomfort, it will bear gifts. The nature of disagreement is discomfort—but discomfort just means that a boundary is being stretched.

What does this mean on a practical level? It means understanding the other person first and taking a position second. If we rush to take a position and say any form of "You are wrong and I am right," the dialogue between us has nowhere to go. If you can express your own feelings *without* making pronouncements about your partner's, you invite greater and greater intimacy. If each can find a way to acknowledge the validity of the other's feelings, there can be a conversation. Even if a couple ends up disagreeing on the specific outcome, they will have evolved their relationship, their knowledge of each other, to a deeper level. And that is seriously what it is all about.

The most essential tool in the answering of questions, both difficult and easy, is kindness. As mentioned, somehow this has been conflated with "nice," but true kindness is an extraordinary combination of soft and hard, simple and complex. It can be held through disagreement, pain, anger, even unkindness—without sacrificing any part of the truth of your feelings, responses, and needs. This sort of kindness enables you to be yourself, to show yourself, and to receive the truth of your beloved, with all their qualities, dear and detested.

True kindness is the ability to open your eyes, ears, mind, and heart to what your beloved is saying and feeling, to who your beloved actually is, rather than who you hoped they would be. In relationships, it seems we will be faced with this choice over and over. Do I choose to pay attention to you or to whom I wish you were? Both are important, don't get me wrong. You should have the love you wish for, but which is more important right now? Each time you choose to step beyond your limits to embrace your partner for who they are rather than who you hoped they would be, something deepens. (I must repeat: this does not include the limits of a partnership that includes abuse or addiction.) On good days, you will be delighted by what you learn. On other days, you may be appalled, disappointed, bored. In each instance it is vital to still listen without denying the truth of what you are hearing out of your own insecurity and fear.

I learned a great lesson in this kind of listening long before I was married, from a man who was my boyfriend at the time. I was quite young and we lived together in a foreign country. I reached a point where I could not decide whether to spend the rest of my life with this person in another country (at the age of nineteen!) or return to my country and begin to build my life there. It was such a painful situation. We really loved each other. We would have long conversations and just hold each other and cry. Then one day he said, "I think you should go home." When I asked what made him say that, he answered, "I love you more than I love us," and, boom, there you have it, a lesson in love for the ages. To love your partner a little bit more than you love your relationship to them may be the kindest thing of all.

To embody this sort of kindness, you have to be in constant, uncompromising contact with your own responses, hopes, and fears. You have to be brave enough to be honest with yourself. Then you can be honest with your partner and able to separate their words from your feelings about them. When discussing the Hard Questions about each other's professional aspirations, for example, your partner may express a desire to leave a boring-but-well-paying job for a more risky but potentially satisfying possibility. This may, understandably, arouse fear for you. Why? Explore the fear and try to differentiate it from the decision facing your partner. Perhaps it brings up concern that the new job will introduce your partner to a new group of people. But, "When you talk about wanting to switch jobs, I'm afraid you'll fall in love with someone else" is different from the normal risk involved in taking a new job. It's incredibly easy to confuse the two. It's important to understand your fear so that you don't discourage your partner's opportunity out of some general, unnamed fear of change. It's equally important that your partner hear in a similarly nonjudgmental way what the potential change elicits in you.

First, there is the awareness of discomfort when the new job is spoken of. That is yours. Then there is the meaning of the new job for your partner. That is theirs. Both are crucial to discuss. For better and worse, there is no rest, no break, no vacation from this discipline of knowing yourself and opening to your loved one. It is not easy, but it is better than "easy"; it's enlivening. This is actually what maintains the heat between you over time.

Once you have fully heard your partner's perspective and considered what they are saying apart from your own needs and reactions, then it is time to let them come flooding in. Speak your truth. It's totally possible to have a thorough conversation about the new job: the pros, cons, logistics, their hopes, and fears—and then say, "Okay, but I absolutely hate this, I am terrified, I can't bear the thought of you making this change in our lives." And then it is their turn to hear you and to receive you. Holding two different vantage points simultaneously can be very complex—but endlessly useful.

Ultimately, what choice do we have in communication that isn't manipulative or unconscious and numb? You speak. You are heard. The other person speaks and is heard. And on it goes. When you have something very difficult and potentially frightening to say to someone you love, you begin by saying, "I have something very difficult and potentially frightening to say," and then you say it. In that sense, communication is really quite simple. Not easy, but straightforward.

For Duncan and myself, our first wedding vow was, "I vow to know you deeply and with compassion." This is the commitment: to know each other and to receive each other. To be known and received. How much I have longed for just this, to be together with my partner in this place of endless relating to the natural ebb and flow of emotion, desire, and evolution. Is this not the ultimate kindness?

Deal-Breaker Questions

Once I received an email from someone who wished *The Hard Questions* had been around when she got married. Why? Because she only discovered that her partner did not want children after they'd been married for about a year. *How could you not know that?* I wondered to myself. But from conversations with her and others, I've seen how easy it is to stay away from certain questions, either because you are afraid of the answer or, more likely, one simply assumes *of course they will want children, who doesn't want children?* Not so fast.

I've talked a lot so far about the questions being more important than the answers, about how it doesn't matter if you agree, disagree, or don't know, as much as it does to simply be honest. However, this is not always true. There may be some questions where, if the answers differ, you may not want to stay together. I know that sounds scary, but, seriously, if this is the case, it is better to know it now rather than a month, year, or decade in. Children are an obvious example as this is one area where it is either a "yes" or a "no" answer. Whatever you decide, at some point, you will not be able to change your mind. So, that's an important one.

For other couples, the question of religion may be a deal breaker. You may think, *Well, once we're married, I'm sure they'll see it my way and become an observant Christian/Jew/pagan because they know how important this is to me.* Not necessarily.

For still others, the question of money can create an unbridgeable gap. You may envision yourself with few possessions, working remotely from wherever you are in order to finance a nomadic existence. Your partner, on the other hand, may want more money to live a less adventurous but more luxurious life.

When you are dating, you may not talk about children, religion, and money. But when you begin to discuss marriage, it is really important to do so.

Before you discuss the Hard Questions with a partner, review them yourself to see which, if any, may be "deal breakers," meaning, if your answers differ, it may be best to break up. Any sentiment that begins with "Once we are married" bears scrutiny. The truth is, once you are married, you will each still be the same person.

If You Get Stuck . . .

. . . or even if you don't, the following technique is a great way to go through the Hard Questions. It is something that I teach when I am leading groups or teaching a class and I have seen over and over how powerful—and simple—it is.

Sit down together, somewhere quiet where you won't be disturbed for fifteen or so minutes. Have a timer handy. Shut off all mobile devices or anything that goes *ping, beep,* or *swoosh*. If said device is to be used as a timer, put it into airplane mode or otherwise take it offline.

You'll take turns answering a particular question, so decide who will speak first and who will listen. Each speaker will have five minutes. Start the timer, and if you are the listener, pose the question.

And then . . . listen. Your partner will speak to the question and they can do so in whatever way they like. They can talk for the entire five minutes. They can cite all the reasons for their answer or express whatever emotions come up around it. They can speak and then be silent. They can be silent and then speak. Whatever they do, the job of the listener is simply to listen. Listen fully. No cross talk, no "Aha," "WTF," "No!!," or "Yes, yes!" All you have to do is make the effort to understand what your partner is saying. If they fall into silence, try to make it comfortable for them to do so by not staring at them or egging them on. At the end, when the timer goes off, all you have to say is one word: "Yes." And then switch.

When the exercise is over, it is up to you what to do. You can debrief, change the subject, take a few minutes of silence to reflect, turn on the TV . . . whatever you like.

The key to this exercise is knowing you will not

be interrupted, so do your best to employ the superpower called "listening."

Some Semi-Surprising Things I've Learned from Talking to Readers Who Have Used the Hard Questions

The book does not include answers—that
surprised some people.

The answers you and your partner have will change
over time and that's okay. (Some have worried that
they will have to sign *The Hard Questions* in blood.)

The questions are super down-to-earth, not
fantasy-based.

The object is to rely on your own wisdom, not on
my (or anyone's) theories and ideas.

It's better to know NOW.

The questions are not just for couples. Single
people have benefited because they have grown
clearer about the partner they desire.

Some people have broken up—and been grateful for it.

The book has been gifted countless times by moms and dads who want their children to make the most informed choices possible.

It may sound unromantic to go through these questions and, for some, it may have been. But I've heard from many people who thought it would be an exercise in logistics but found instead that they fell even more deeply in love.

And the most frequently asked question, the one I've heard over and over, from people of all ages and all stages of relationship is this one:

———

Q: *What if I want to answer these questions but my partner does not? How can I get them to do so?*

A: If your intended will not discuss issues related to home, children, money, and so on with you, now . . . what makes you think they ever will? The truth is, these questions are going to come up anyway. Better to answer them now, during peacetime, rather than later, in battle. If you're being asked to make a commitment without knowing what that commitment entails, well, I'm not a lawyer, but in every other area of life, that would be considered illegal.

———

As far as "getting" someone to want to have a conversation—there is no way to do so that I know of. Even if you threatened, cajoled, seduced, insisted, made it lighthearted, you're not a parent trying to get a kid to do homework. You're discussing one of the most important steps you can ever take, one that changes everything. You're offering your heart for another's keeping and volunteering to do the same for them. It's just not something you want to go into blind.

This book is for anyone desiring a lasting marriage who also wants a relationship that will continue to deepen—and is brave enough to invite the self-knowledge that fuels honesty and welcome the

same from their partner. Self-knowledge is insepa-
rable from intimacy; as one deepens, so does the
other. My belief is this may be the only kind of
relationship that can succeed, that can weather the
storms and ride out the eddies, that can be ardent
and secure, all at once.

CHAPTER ONE

———♡———

Home

I am very introverted and prefer to have lots of time alone. (I also don't have kids, which makes this even remotely possible.) This is not easy for Duncan. Once when we were having a very intense argument (about I honestly can't remember what), he sputtered, "The most important thing in my life is us. The most important thing in your life is you." I was about to sputter something hurtful back, but when I opened my mouth, what came out was, "You're right." I mean, it's not that I'm selfish (except when I am), but my inner world is what gets most of my attention. On good days, this results in writing helpful books or discovering something useful about why things are the way they are. Duncan, on the other hand, is super-relational. He genuinely gets more enjoyment out of doing something together. I enjoy things more when I do them by myself. I'm really serious about this privacy thing. We lived apart for the first three years of our marriage, I in New York City and he in Boston. (That's a long story, good for another time.) When we talked about creating a home together, to be honest, I thought it would be awesome to keep living apart. When we were together, we could devote all our time and attention to each other and when we were apart, we could devote all our time and attention to the other important things in our lives. To me, that sounded ideal. However, there was someone for whom this did not sound ideal, and that was Duncan. (P.S. Also: EXPENSIVE.) He wanted to live together because, for him, that meant greater intimacy. I preferred more separation for the same reason.

When the hassles and dollars became too much,

I moved to Boston and we began to discuss the home we would create. His attention was on shared space and, unsurprisingly, mine was on having a separate space, whether it was a nook or a spare bedroom. The truth is, both are important, having a shared environment *and* a personal environment that suits you. Usually, however, one of those aspects is important to one of you while the second is more important to the other. The problem comes in when we refuse to recognize the validity of our partner's preferences.

Our home is the most immediate expression of who we are and how we view life. It is the place we retire to after giving of ourselves in the world all day long, even if we work at home. It is the one place in the world that should be a safe space. It is the location, for many, of what-we-do-besides-work, i.e., hobbies and creative endeavors; the pursuit of dreams that may have nothing to do with work-aday efforts to secure income and achieve status; the place where we long to unfold, be ourselves, show the world who we are, and share our lives with those we love most. In addition, home is the most tangible manifestation of financial and emotional security. Too, for many, the question of ease and finding a welcoming community is beyond important—it is essential.

Marriage often begins with agreeing to share a home—to share the financial commitment to maintain it, the joys and hassles of furnishing it, the creation of a way of living together. After the ceremony, after the honeymoon (if there is one), the newlyweds *go home*. Even if they lived together before, this particular trip home is different. *Now we are a family. Now we are here to stay. Now my things are also yours. Or are they? Now your clothes on the floor mean something different . . . is this what I will come home to every day?* Things that irritate you before marriage can terrify you after.

The space you and your partner will share is central to the establishment of an "us" in addition to "me" and "you." Form can give rise to content. No matter how much you love each other, the feeling and properties—and location—of the space you share can affect the course of your relationship. A small space may feel cozy to you but suffocating to your partner. Casual housekeeping may denote relaxation to your partner and slovenliness to you. Your partner may appreciate your love of beauty or be threatened by it. And in addition to questions about the feeling and vibe of the inner space, there is the whole question of geography. Where will the home be located? For many couples, us included, that has not been a simple question to answer.

Physical space may mirror the way psychological space is delineated. Do you require a lot of privacy, separate from your partner? Will finances or square footage allow for it, if so? Do you need space to work from home? Is it important to you to dine together? Host parties? Celebrate holidays? What your home looks like, how much time is required to care for it, how much of your income goes into creating and sustaining it, whether it is important or not to own your home, where it is located, even if you will share a single home—the answers to these questions reflect deeply held assumptions about life, the future, and what makes it all meaningful for you. We often begin envisioning our homes when we are still small children. "When I'm grown, my house will have a swimming pool in every room" may have morphed into "I want a big bathtub"—but still, that tub may be emblematic of a long-held desire. It's good to uncover and share these desires, no matter how unlikely they may appear in the cool light of adulthood. And remember: Your home is where you live with your partner, but it is also where *you* live. Whether or not you have the luxury of space, your home needs to shelter both the couple and each individual in meaningful ways.

These questions will help the two of you to clarify your views of home and home life.

1. What does our home look like, physically? Outside? Inside? Any particular style (modern, traditional, etc.)?

2. Do we hope to own our home (if we do not currently) or do we envision a more nomadic life? Do we prefer renting to owning? Now? In five years? Ten?

3. Where can we make a home that will feel secure to us? Where we will feel welcomed, included, and comfortable raising our children (should we have them)?

4. How do we each feel about the impact of our actions on the environment? What is important to each of us regarding environmental concerns and sustainability? How committed are we each to doing our part to protect the planet and how is that reflected in the choices we make about our home, if at all?

5. What is important for me/us to be able to do at home (relax, work, make love, study, meditate, play guitar, be with friends)?

6. Describe the feeling you want to have when you walk into our home. What makes you feel secure, happy?

7. How much time do we imagine spending online during a typical evening? Weekend? Are we okay with bringing our mobile devices everywhere, or do we want to set limits (like, at the dinner table or while in bed)?

8. Do either of us have a relationship with video games and online gaming in general, and, if so, how does the other feel about it?

9. Are either or both of us active on social media? Do either of us want to place limits on what is to be shared online of our personal and home life? If so, what are they?

10. Where is our home? Describe its ideal geographical location. What surrounds the house? Neighbors? Trees? Shops and restaurants? The ocean? A gated community? Acres of undeveloped land?

11. What is it? Apartment? House? Town house? RV?

12. Who is responsible for keeping our house clean and organized and our yard (if relevant) cared for? Are we different in terms of our needs for cleanliness and/or organization? Is one or both of us neat? Messy? A pack rat? An organizational wizard? How will we divide housecleaning responsibilities?

13. Who is responsible for grocery shopping, cooking, and other tasks connected with meals? Do we eat out? A lot? A little? Do we eat meals together?

14. What percentage of our income are we prepared to spend to rent or purchase and maintain our home on a monthly or annual basis? Or will we live with family or friends at first?

15. Do we have a budget for decorating our home? If so, what is it? What factors are important in making these decisions (price, quality, style)? How will we make decisions together?

16. Do we have a sense of our own style? Do we care? What is my style? Yours? Ours?

17. How long will we live in our current home or homes (if we live separately)? One year? Ten years? Forever?

18. In terms of sleep habits, are we "morning people" or "night people"? Light or heavy sleepers? Do either of us work nights or early mornings or otherwise have need for special consideration around sleep?

19. Who might also stay there or live there? Do we have any roommates or tenants?

20. Do we have (or want) a pet? If one of us has a pet now, how will that pet become part of our life together?

21. Will we live together? (This may seem like an odd question, but some couples who want—or need—to do so are living separately, whether due to personal preference or geographic need.)

22. If we're approaching retirement, might we want to move? If so, where and when?

23. Will we need to sell our current home in order to retire?

24. How do we feel about guests? In particular, how do we feel about having in-laws stay with us? Siblings? Other family members?

25. What if our parent(s) need to move in full time?

26. Are both of us open to seeking marital counseling if it were necessary? What if one of us isn't?

—♡—

CHAPTER TWO

Money

Of all the subjects couples can discuss, money may be the most intense, complex, and consequential of all. It is among the most important topics couples should address together, and yet is the one least likely to be discussed openly. Money can mean security, love, power, and/or freedom. Perhaps because of its various levels of meaning, it is one of the subjects most battled over, in part because we are so hesitant to discuss it that, once we finally do, we may be surprised at what we find. It's really important to take off the blinders and *look*. It is almost guaranteed that each partner holds assumptions about money, from "If I stay home to care for our kids, you will support us" to "Separate bank accounts indicate mistrust" or "If I make more money than you, I get more decision-making power about our lives." These are serious assumptions with the capacity to change the fabric of life and the meaning of marriage altogether.

It behooves you to examine them all—but almost everyone I know cringes at the thought of discussing money. I know more about my friends' sex lives than I do about their bank accounts. Money can be a source of shame or aggression. It can communicate love or disdain. It can support or undercut self-esteem. It can be used as a helpful tool or a hurtful weapon.

Our Western culture (at least as of this writing) is governed by consumerist values. While religion, politics, relationships, nature, and culture may matter (or not) to you, our lives are not built around them as much as they are around financial imperatives and the drive to acquire. I'm not saying it is wrong to want a bunch of money or have beautiful things. Personally, I want both. However, if we fail to see that our world is constructed around money, we may not be seeing clearly and it is important to investigate our own and our partner's fears, beliefs, and hopes.

Growing up, I had no idea how much money my family had (or did not have). We never talked about it—and yet we talked about it all the time. "That's too expensive." "Money does not grow on trees." "Save as much as possible because it could all fall apart." "I'm giving you twenty dollars for your birthday." "Look at their home, they must be rich." And so on. But somehow, it never seemed quite real. I am still learning about money, how to earn, invest, spend, and save it. I suspect I'm not alone because money is one of the most terrifying subjects of all and the one most likely to drive our actions without our awareness.

Marriage intensifies financial hopes, dreams, and fears. Even today, for some women, no matter how independent, there is an expectation of being cared for financially. For some men, a culturally ingrained sense of needing to provide and take care of family comes to the surface. There is nothing wrong with these expectations; the only problem is if you don't know these things about yourself or your partner and one or both of you move forward with hidden agendas. The great unconscious cultural archetypes—women provided for, men providing—manifest with special intensity on the way to the bank. Again, there is no criticism of these archetypes. They can be just right, as long as both of you are aware of them. Problems arise when one model ("We are equally responsible for our finances") is expressed, while another model ("Take care of me/I am in charge of the money") is *felt*.

The following questions may actually seem impolite or grabby. THEY ARE NOT. They're just practical—and, if you don't know the answers when you hitch your lives together, you may have missed discussing the single most important foundation for an honest, true partnership. So, don't be shy.

1. How much money do we each have right now? In checking accounts? Savings accounts? Investments, annuities, retirement funds?

2. How much debt do we each have? Include everything: school or business loans, personal loans, credit cards. Will we combine this debt once we're married?

3. Do you know your net worth and, if so, what is it?

4. Where do we each keep our money currently?

5. Do you have any past or current financial boons or busts that I should know about?

6. How much money do we earn together right now? How much do we hope to earn in one year? Five years? Ten years? How will we get to these numbers, as best we can say right now?

7. What do we project our expenses to be per month? For the next year?

8. What are our categories of expense (rent/mortgage, insurance, food)? How much do we spend monthly, annually, in each category? How much do we want to be able to spend? Now? In one year? Five years?

Is our current combined income enough to cover those expenses?

9. What are our financial goals for one year from now? Five years? Ten years?

10. How much money should be in our savings account so that each of us feels "safe"? How much, if any, do we contribute to it monthly or annually? Who makes these contributions, and in what proportion? What if our financial goals are vastly different?

11. Do we have similar ideologies on how money should be saved? Is one of us significantly more frugal than the other?

12. Where do we put our money (bank account, mutual funds, retirement plans)?

13. Do we keep our money in joint or individual accounts?

14. Will we share credit cards?

15. What kinds of purchases must be jointly decided upon?

16. How do we decide how to spend our money? Is there an amount ($50, $500, $5,000) over which we need to discuss a purchase before committing to it?

17. How do we keep the household books and pay bills?

18. How do we manage long-range financial planning (retirement, investments)? How are these decisions made and who implements/tracks/manages them? Is life insurance secured? In what amounts? Who are the beneficiaries? Do we need or want to include care for aging relatives in our plans?

19. Do we have preexisting investments and, if so, will any changes be necessary after marriage?

20. If we have dependents from a previous relationship, what part of our finances goes to them, now and in the future? When unpredicted financial events occur involving them, what is the new spouse's involvement/input/responsibility?

21. Do we each have health insurance? If not, how is health insurance secured? How may any of this change after marriage? Do either of us have existing health needs, concerns, or conditions?

22. If we want to retire, how much money do we need in savings before giving up our jobs?

23. Do you have a will? If so, what does it say and will any changes be made after we are married? If not, should we arrange to have one? Jointly or separately?

24. Do we have or need a financial advisor to help us manage our finances and achieve our goals?

CHAPTER THREE

♡

Work

Work can be the center of our lives or simply the means to an end, or both. In any case, outside of family, our most important relationships may be at work. We may spend more time with colleagues than with each other. Professional relationships and goals can have a powerful impact on the life of a couple. You and your partner may have quite specific views of the role of your work in your personal life and the role you envision your partner's work might have. For example, "My partner will never/always have to work." "My partner's work will never/always support us." "My travel and time needs for work will/will not take precedence over family commitments." And so on. It's important to examine these assumptions together.

Most likely, both partners will require each other's emotional and/or financial support to reach their work goals. Perhaps you expect your partner to understand that you will sometimes have to prioritize time at work over time spent together. Perhaps you think your work is more important on some level (because it is more financially or creatively meaningful, or more charitable) than your partner's. You may think work should take place between 9:00 and 5:00 and be forgotten about otherwise, or you may work according to a less structured rhythm. One may view work as a necessary evil while the other may hold work as a means of self-expression.

None of these views are incorrect. The only problem is not knowing (or appreciating) your partner's relationship to work.

Answering the questions below can help you and your partner clarify feelings about such important topics as ambition, expectations of support, the meaning of work for each of you, and expectations of support and commitment to your own and your partner's professional goals.

1. What are our separate professional goals in terms of position or job desired? One year from now? Five years? Fifteen years?

2. Is each of us content with our current jobs? If not, why?

3. How much time will each of us spend working, and during what hours? Do we begin work early? Will we prefer to work into the evening?

4. Do you understand my relationship to my work? Do you understand what my work means to me in terms of time, effort, and/or creative self-expression?

5. How ambitious am I? How ambitious are you? Are we each comfortable with the other's level of ambition?

6. How do I wish you would support my professional/work goals? Do I need time and space to explore my creativity? Do I need financial support? Do I need your advice? Do I need time and money to attend school or receive additional professional training?

7. When, if ever, do we each want to retire?

CHAPTER FOUR

Health and Food

Attitudes toward food and the ways we eat, shop, prepare, and serve it can reflect deeper values, and so can attitudes toward exercise, fitness, and what it means to live a healthy life, feel good in our bodies, and age well. For some couples, food is actually a central part of the relationship and they may enjoy cooking together, dining together, and/or going out to eat. Meals may be a source of relaxation, a time to catch up, and a source of delight. Some people find food and the act of dining together to be one of the great sensual joys of life. Good food, drink, and conversation are time-honored sources of pleasure. Others consider such things to be a nuisance, an expense, inexplicably complex. There can be great satisfaction in being very formal or very casual about food. I know happy couples who make sure to always have dinner together. I know equally happy couples who never dine together unless they are going out. There are no right answers here.

In addition, the way we prepare and eat food bears direct relation to the way we feel about and take care of our health. When you are sick, what foods make you feel cared for? Do you have opinions about what to eat to maintain health, immunity, vitality? The way we feed and care for ourselves and others, in sickness and in health, speaks loud and clear about what makes us feel nurtured. When I was sick as a child, my mother would bring me toast and tea. To this day toast and tea make me feel better, no matter what I may have learned in the interim about caffeine and glycemic indices.

For most of us, eating treads the line between science and art. We may find it very important to adhere to a certain diet out of ethical, cultural, or religious beliefs, or for purposes of weight management, cancer prevention, enhancing energy, or controlling a chronic health condition. We may consider the act of preparing and eating food to be an expression of pure delight, or feel that paying attention to the quality and preparation of food is a sign of hopeless narcissism or new age propaganda. What delights me may feel onerous to you and vice versa, of course.

Exercise and fitness are also important, I think we can all agree—but that is where the agreement ends. Some of us exercise for mental health and balance, some out of dissatisfaction with how we look, to gain weight, lose weight, retain vigor, or manage chronic health conditions. Some people find joy and meaning in fitness while others, well, do not. Some want to exercise every day and some want to exercise on no day. For some, going to the gym or for a walk or hike together is a part of the relationship. For others, not so much. It is helpful to think about how your attitudes may differ, and what conflicts may arise over issues of wellness as time goes on.

1. Do we eat meals together? Which ones?

2. Who is responsible for food shopping?

3. Do we both like to cook? Neither? Do we like each other's cooking?

4. Do either of us have special dietary concerns or needs relating to health? Does the other agree with or support these needs?

5. How much time do we spend exercising? How much time do we want to spend?

6. Do we each feel comfortable about our current levels of fitness and health? Are there any areas of concern to one or both of us?

7. Does either of us have health concerns (e.g.,

chronic conditions such as high blood pressure, diabetes, or asthma) that run in the family?

8. Do the health, dietary, and/or exercise needs of one or both of us require any lifestyle adjustments or changes? Any special financial expenditures?

9. Do we each feel supported by the other in these areas?

10. Is each of us happy with our overall health? Where could there be improvements?

11. Is each of us happy with the other's approach to health? Does one have habits or tendencies that concern the other (e.g., smoking, excessive dieting, unhealthful food choices)?

12. How do we meet in the middle if our eating habits/diets are different (e.g., vegan versus carnivore)? How will we then determine how we should feed our children, if we have them?

13. Do either of us have a history of addiction to drugs or alcohol, either personal or within our family of origin?

Do either of us have concerns about the other's use of drugs or alcohol?

14. Do we have any strong feelings about consumption of drugs or alcohol in our home? Will we serve or drink alcohol at home?

CHAPTER FIVE

——♡——

Family

When dating, you may or may not have in-depth conversations about each other's relationships with parents, siblings, and/or each other's children— but when you marry, those relationships take on a different meaning. They can reveal a lot about your values. I may believe that all family members should be welcome in our house at any time of day or night, while my partner may feel that we should discuss if and when an invitation should be issued first, even if a family member is in crisis. You may feel that you should drop everything to support a family member and I may feel otherwise, either because it would impact us negatively, I don't particularly like that family member, or I also need you. I may wish to consult my mother over certain issues; my partner may view this as intrusive or overly dependent.

Most of us retain into adulthood unresolved issues with our families of origin—issues that we may attempt to resolve, consciously or not, within the context of marriage. If you have a parent who is an alcoholic, for example, you may refuse to keep liquor in your home, but your partner may enjoy having a drink with dinner. Can you (or should you) separate your deep feelings about alcohol from your partner's preferences?

Families are complicated and may involve parents, siblings, half-siblings, stepchildren, ex-spouses, extended families, and long distances. Whether a family is nuclear or fragmented (or both), ferocious feelings may be provoked by one partner's criticism, judgments, or expectations of the other's family. It's important to look carefully at the dynamics in both partners' families of origin and think clearly about what it means to create a family together.

1. What about my family of origin supports me? Us? What does not?

2. What do you like about my family of origin? What do you dislike?

3. What is your current relationship to my family? Are you close? Do you desire more or less closeness? Do they desire more closeness from you? Are you comfortable with my parents, siblings, and relatives?

4. What do you need me to know about your culture and family of origin? What will help me to connect and are there any issues we could anticipate together?

5. What place does the other's family play in our family life? How often do we visit or socialize

together? If we have out-of-town relatives, will we ask them to visit us for extended periods? Can they stay at our home? How often? For what length of time?

6. If we have children, what kind of relationship do we hope our parents will have to their grandchildren? How much time will they spend together?

7. What holidays and events do we feel are important to spend with our family of origin? Do we give gifts? Do we have special celebrations? If so, what is involved and where are the celebrations held?

8. What holidays and events are important for our family to observe? How do we celebrate and what kind of time is spent celebrating each other's birthdays? Our anniversary? Our children's birthdays? Our relatives' birthdays, anniversaries, and special events?

9. What might we do should our parents or

other family members become ill and need us to care for them? Support them financially? Provide them with shelter?

10. How important is it to live close to your family of origin?

CHAPTER SIX

—♡—

Children

One of my most beloved friends had children late in life, in her forties. It is always a massive life change to have children, but the energy demands may feel different to a twenty-two-year-old than to a forty-two-year-old. She and her partner were so happy to have had a child, they thanked their lucky stars every day and doted on their baby. They also had the requisite sleepless nights and worries about teething and so on. They were good about sharing the middle-of-the-night duties, but one night when she expected her partner to take his turn getting up to see to the baby but he did not, she dragged herself out of bed, walked over to the crib, turned on the light, screamed "FUCK YOU," and walked out. Okay, this youngster is now about to graduate high school and is as well loved and well adjusted as anyone I have ever known. I'm not sharing this anecdote to indicate anything other than the crazy pressure that comes with parenting.

I know some couples who have agreed never to have children. I know others who want them right away. I have known some who have felt strongly one way or the other and then changed their minds. This is hardly surprising, since few decisions in life are as important as whether or not to have children—and if so, when.

Childless couples hear all sorts of stories from their friends who are new parents: "We are completely sleep-deprived." "We never have sex anymore." "We had no idea what it would mean to love someone this much." "We can't stand to be away from our baby, even to go to work." "Our baby is driving us crazy/we are completely in love with her." It sounds trite to say so, but having a baby is the most common thing in the world (I mean, we all got here that way)—yet nothing can prepare you for life as parents.

Friends of mine in their late thirties became pregnant while on their honeymoon. They definitely wanted to have children and knew that time was not on their side. While they were ecstatic to learn of their pregnancy, they also really missed having time to acclimate to life together as partners. In your relationship, do you want to have plenty of time to get to know each other and establish a household before having children? Do you want to have children right away? If nature allows, it's wonderful to consider such questions while you still have the ability to make choices.

Some years ago, this very book was featured on the *Oprah Winfrey Show.* I was invited on as a guest to discuss how the book came about, but that was by no means the highlight of the episode. The Oprah crew had invited four couples to actually ask the Hard Questions and then come on the show to discuss what it was like. Three of the four couples wrestled beautifully with the process and came out the other side more committed to each other. They were quite happy with the result. The fourth couple? They broke up because one *did not know* that the other did not want to have children. Yes, it was quite sad to see their relationship end, but I think they, too, were happy with the result because they found out about this massive difference before the wedding rather than after. (Hey, you *Oprah* couples! Hope you're all well!)

Another friend once said to me, "Having a child brings you face-to-face with the best and worst of yourself." Both she and her partner are exhausted by the demands of their beloved year-old baby. My friend is testing the limits of her patience, selflessness, and energy—as well as the limits of her relationship. In addition to lifestyle changes, questions about raising and caring for children can evoke primal and perhaps half-consciously held opinions about health, religion, discipline, education, and family. Many logistical and philosophical questions arise about providing childcare; teaching values; establishing routines for eating, playing, and schoolwork; instilling religious or spiritual beliefs; and administering discipline. Let's face it, there could be a whole book of questions *just* about having children. While it is impossible to anticipate exactly how you will feel when you have children, it is useful to prepare for it by discussing beliefs about raising them. And if you decide you don't want children, it may be useful also to discuss how you will respond to questions asked by friends, relatives, and even strangers.

1. Will we have children together?

2. If so, when?

3. How many?

4. How important is having children to each of us?

5. What is our best path to becoming parents?

Are there issues of fertility, surrogacy, adoption, or other topics we should discuss?

6. How will having a child change the way we live now? Will we want or be able to take time off from work, or work a reduced schedule? For how long? In the months or years following the birth of our child, will we need to rethink who is responsible for housekeeping and other aspects of managing our life together?

7. When our child is older, will we try to enforce any particular dietary habits (limit sweets, prohibit processed foods, encourage vegetarianism, etc.)?

8. How will we instill discipline in our child? Lectures? Yelling? Time-outs? Is one of us more naturally a disciplinarian? How will we handle our disagreements over administering discipline and teaching manners and values?

9. What are our parenting styles? How will we co-parent if our styles differ?

10. Who will take care of our child if we both work?

11. When our child is older, will we limit access to TV, music, computers, or reading materials based on content? What type of content do we find objectionable? What sort of TV, music, computer games, Internet content, or reading materials will we encourage or discourage? Will we set time or viewing limits on TV? On time spent playing video games or surfing the Internet?

12. Will we raise our children with any particular religious or spiritual beliefs? If so, how will we do this? Will we give our children a religious education or expect them to participate in religious rituals (observance of Sabbath, religious holidays, confirmations, Bar/Bat Mitzvah, etc.)? What will we teach our children about big issues such as God? Suffering? Birth? Death?

13. How important is it to us to expose our children to different ethnicities, cultural backgrounds, and/or religions? What actionable steps will we take to raise tolerant children and teach them about racial, religious, and social injustice?

15. Do we have expectations about what we want our children to be/do? Is that important to us? What do we define as "success" for our children?

16. If we decide not to have children, are we both completely comfortable with the decision? What if one of us changes our mind? What conversations might we expect to have (or avoid) with relatives or friends about our decision?

Regarding children from previous relationships:

1. How much time will we all spend together?

2. What does the birth parent expect in terms of their child's relation to the stepparent? What does the stepparent expect? What role, if any, will the stepparent play in the care, discipline, and education of their partner's child?

3. What is the child's physical and emotional space in the new family and home? What special care needs to be taken to assure their comfort and security in the birth parent's new relationship?

4. What will the children call the stepparent?

5. If one or both partners' children are grown and parenting issues aren't relevant, what role will each play in the lives of these grown children, if any? What emotional or psychological issues might we anticipate in relation to our own or our partner's grown children?

6. Regarding our grown children, what events or holidays are they accustomed to spending with their parent? Will we continue that tradition as a family?

CHAPTER SEVEN

___♡___

Community and Friends

One of the great complaints about modern life is lack of community. Whereas our parents or grandparents were more likely to have been born into a community, these days most of us have to consciously create one. A contemporary couple's life is often full of micro-communities, based around work, fitness, hobbies, creative pursuits, or spirituality. Community can also come from specific friendships: With these people we do sports; with these we talk about books; with these we have parties. Both partners bring to the relationship a set of existing friendships: new, historic, dysfunctional, meaningful.

Because it's not always easy for your partner to naturally fit into the other's existing communities, it is valuable to take a look at them one by one and see where the possibilities for deeper community or the risk of distress lie.

1. With whom do we socialize as a couple?

2. How do we meet new people, if we would like to?

3. Are we satisfied with the friendships we currently have? Would we like to be more involved socially? Are we overwhelmed socially, and do we need to cut back on such commitments?

4. What issues, if any, do we anticipate in attempting to fit in with each other's pre-existing communities? What do we need to discuss? What do you want me to know/avoid/accept?

5. If one or both of us have been married before, are there friendships that we shared as a couple with our previous spouse that we'd like to maintain? Together or separately?

6. What kind of community do we envision ourselves in? Close-knit? Occasional get-togethers? Based around work, religion, cultural pursuits, or hobbies? How do we achieve that community?

7. Which of us is responsible for creating community? Is one partner more outgoing than the other?

8. Does one partner have a greater need for outside friendships and groups?

9. Do I appreciate/resent the way my partner interacts with my friends? Of my existing friendships, do any seem particularly wonderful or threatening to my partner?

CHAPTER EIGHT

————♡————

Society

When this book was first published, there was less need for a chapter such as this, one that addresses issues of politics, service, and environment. When I got married, it was not uncommon for a couple to belong to different political parties. They may have disagreed on many things, but it was not seen in the polarizing light that it is held in today. It is so heartbreaking to see that this is what we have come to, at least in the United States. I long for the day when we can once again look at each other across the political divide with utterly divergent opinions—and respect. May that day come quickly. In the meantime . . .

In addition to questions about politics, since the first edition of this book was published, environmental concerns have become urgent. I can't even imagine what questions we will need to ask ourselves in the future, but for now, it is vital to examine our feelings and beliefs about environmental footprint, sustainability, and care for the planet. Our future depends upon it.

1. Do we share a political ideology? If so, what is it? Does it matter to you who I vote for?

2. If not, do we imagine a time when this could present a problem?

3. If so, is it important to take action to support that ideology, whether through volunteering, attending meetings, running for office, or offering financial support?

4. Do either of us have friends or family who

support a political or social ideology that runs counter to what we believe? If so, how do we imagine relating to them separately and together?

5. How much do we each prioritize environmental concerns? What habits are important to us to combat global warming?

6. Do we each understand best practices for creating a sustainable home, however we may define sustainability?

7. Do we feel comfortable in our existing social groups: seen, included, and valued? If not, what can we do about it?

8. If we are from different racial, economic, or cultural backgrounds, are we able to understand each other's reality sufficiently to feel seen and known? If not, what would you like me to see that I currently do not?

9. Are we comfortable giving each other feedback when we say or do racially or socially insensitive things?

10. Are there things we can or want to do to create a more righteous world for all?

11. Do we currently belong to or support (with money and/or time) any movements or causes? Would we like to make this more of a focus in our life together?

CHAPTER NINE

———♡———

Spirituality

For some of us, religion is at the very center of daily life and our beliefs inform choices about where we live, how we spend our time, and whom we associate with. For others, if anything, religion is something that we observe when someone is born, marries, or dies. At such times, whether we think of ourselves as religious or not, the traditions your family may have followed can become suddenly important. Any impulse your beloved may have to devalue or ignore such traditions can become extremely hurtful. It's important to examine what you will do, if anything, to mark the passages of life, including death. After all, many marriage vows include the phrase "till death do us part." It is likely that, as much as you will travel together through life, you will also travel together toward death. I know it is no fun to think such thoughts. But part of the sacred trust of committed partnership includes caring for each other in all phases and cycles of life. So, don't be chicken.

In addition to traditional religious beliefs, whether it is through yoga, meditation, or exploring various wisdom traditions, for many, spirituality has become increasingly central in our day-to-day lives. Is it important to share such practices with your partner? If so, why? If not, why not? And what happens when one partner holds a particular religious or spiritual tradition dear and the other does not? Is it possible for it all to be honored under one roof—or not?

1. Do we share a religion? Do we belong to a church, synagogue, mosque, or temple? As a couple? Individually?

2. Do we share a spiritual practice such as meditation, yoga, or some other type of non-traditional observance? If not, is that okay with each of us?

3. Does one of us have an individual spiritual practice? Does each partner understand and respect the other's choices?

4. What does each desire of the other in terms of support and/or participation in religion or spiritual practice?

5. How do we mark births and deaths within our family?

6. Is prayer a part of our home life? If so, how? When? What?

7. Do we observe any spiritual rituals? Celebrate religious holidays? Together? Separately? What role does faith play in our household?

8. How would we like our life and death to be celebrated?

AFTERWORD

♡

A kaleidoscope (kuh-lahy-duh-skohp) is an optical in-strument with two or more reflecting surfaces tilted to each other in an angle.

Some Random Things I've Noticed:

One of you will want to spend more time together. The other will want to spend more time apart.

One of you will care a lot about how to do certain everyday things (i.e., the best way to wash dishes) and the other will not care.

One of you will want to talk about things. The other will prefer to let them lie.

One of you will be more attuned to the present. The other, to the future.

One of you will find arguing helpful and important, will recover quickly from said argument, and think the matter has been resolved. The other will not find it helpful, recover quickly, or find resolution.

One will value relationships over individuality. The other will feel the opposite.

Each of these positions is context-based and subject to reversal at a moment's notice . . . so don't become too certain about who this wonderful, mysterious, infuriating, enlivening person is—or even what relationships are. Eschew labels (anything that begins with "you always . . ." should be avoided at all costs).

The call to stretch beyond your comfort level is always knocking on the door. Who you think you are, ideas about who your partner is, what relationships "should" look like, even what you think you need—none are solid. Rather than looking at your beloved and your relationship through a telescope, it is more helpful to imagine you are looking through a kaleidoscope—and just like a kaleidoscope, to figure out what it is a picture of is not the point; the joy comes from experiencing the display.

Entering marriage can be a commitment to an ever-expanding view of what it means to love and be loved or an unnatural limiting of self. Sometimes it is both. "With you, I will become who I truly am" is much more passionate and courageous than "In order to make you happy, I will narrow who I may become, and try to fit your picture of who I should be." In any case, the latter promise can never be kept. It must shatter. The former is not the commitment to love forever, but the commitment to *act lovingly* forever. This is a profound and worthy commitment, honest and full of grace.

I hope that answering the Hard Questions together with your partner has helped you make a commitment that will last a lifetime. May you live in love and be transformed by it.

ACKNOWLEDGMENTS

♡

A book appears to be a solid creation, but just as matter is crafted by particles, this work is the sum total of wisdom and love received. With profound thanks to my family, my departed father (the embodiment of love itself) Julius Piver, Louise Piver, Carol Hanna, Allison Hanna, Ed Korn, David Piver and Julie Myers, and Forrest Piver. Special thanks to Gabi Browne and Andrew Ermogenous for offering feedback as they contemplate their own marriage. May you live in love! Much gratitude to my guides in love, Rich and Antra Borofsky and Barry Sternfeld. To my heart-friends, Michael Carroll,

Crystal Gandrud, Jenna Hollenstein, Christine Kane, Christopher Kilmer, Joel Marcus, Lisa Morris, Eden Steinberg, and Kevin Townley, and to my treasured sister-colleagues at the Open Heart Project, Lisa Fehl and Kaysha Patel, thank you for your kindness and brilliance. Warm and heartfelt thanks to Ericka Phillips for her insight and wisdom, which made this a better book. I'm grateful to Richard Pine for stepping back in and to Sara Carder for being an editor who shared and expanded my vision. Thank you for being such fun to work with.

With special and inexpressible thanks to Sam Bercholz for his impeccable guidance and to Tulku Thondup Rinpoche for his perfect heart of unconditional love.

And of course, to Duncan, my rock, with gratitude for embarking on this compass-less journey with me.

ABOUT THE AUTHOR

Susan Piver is the *New York Times* bestselling author of many books, including *The Wisdom of a Broken Heart* and *The Four Noble Truths of Love*. She is a meditation teacher and founder of the Open Heart Project, an online mindfulness community with members all over the world. You can reach her at openheartproject.com.

Additional resources for answering the Hard Questions can be found at openheartproject .com/thq.